SCRIPTURE AND TRADITION

SCRIPTURE AND TRADITION

Lutherans and Catholics in Dialogue IX

Edited by
Harold C. Skillrud
J. Francis Stafford
Daniel F. Martensen

MINNEAPOLIS

SCRIPTURE AND TRADITION
Lutherans and Catholics in Dialogue IX

Cover design: Judy Swanson

Library of Congress Cataloging-in-Publication Data

Scripture and tradition / edited by Harold C. Skillrud, J. Francis
    Stafford, and Daniel F. Martensen.
       p.   cm. -- (Lutherans and Catholics in dialogue : 9)
    Includes bibliographical references.
    ISBN 0-8066-2711-5 :
    1. Bible--Evidences, authority, etc. 2. Tradition (Theology)
3. Lutheran Church--Relations--Catholic Church. 4. Catholic Church--
Relations--Lutheran Church. I. Skillrud, Harold C. (Harold
Clayton), 1928-   . II. Stafford, J. Francis, 1932-
III. Martensen, Daniel F.   IV. Series.
BT89.S35   1994
231'.042--dc20   95-47947
                                                    CIP

The paper used in this publication meets the minimum requirements of American National Standard for Information Sciences—Permanence of Paper for Printed Library Materials, ANSI Z329.48-1984.   (∞)™

Manufactured in the U.S.A.   AF 9-2711

99   98   97   96   95   1   2   3   4   5   6   7   8   9   10

Joseph Andrew Sittler   1904–1987
Jerome D. Quinn   1927–1988
Carl J. Peter   1932–1991
Fred Kramer   1902–1991
✠ T. Austin Murphy   1911–1991
Ut Omnes Unum Sint

Contents

Abbreviations

DOCUMENTS OF LUTHERANS AND CATHOLICS IN DIALOGUE

L/RC 1   *The Status of the Nicene Creed as Dogma of the Church* (1965)
L/RC 2   *One Baptism for the Remission of Sins* (1966)
L/RC 3   *The Eucharist as Sacrifice* (1967)
L/RC 4   *Eucharist and Ministry* (1970)
L/RC 5   *Papal Primacy and the Universal Church* (Minneapolis: Augsburg, 1974)
L/RC 6   *Teaching Authority and Infallibility in the Church* (Minneapolis: Augsburg, 1980)
L/RC 7   *Justification by Faith* (Minneapolis: Augsburg, 1985)
L/RC 8   *The One Mediator, the Saints, and Mary* (Minneapolis: Augsburg, 1992)

Vols. 1–4 were originally published by the Bishops' Committee for Ecumenical and Interreligious Affairs, Washington, D.C., and the U.S.A. National Committee of the Lutheran World Federation, New York, N.Y. Vols. 1–3 have been reprinted together in one volume by Augsburg (Minneapolis: n.d.), as has vol. 4 (1979).

VATICAN COUNCIL II

Latin and English versions of the documents of Vatican II may be found in *The Decrees of the Ecumenical Councils*, 2 vols., ed. Norman P. Tanner (Washington, D.C.: Georgetown University Press, 1990).

OTHER ABBREVIATIONS

AAS	*Acta Apostolicae Sedis*
AG	*Ad Gentes*, Vatican II
Ap	*Apology of the Augsburg Confession*, BC
BC	*The Book of Concord. The Confessions of the Evangelical Lutheran Church*, trans. and ed. Theodore G. Tappert (Philadelphia: Fortress, 1959)
BS	*Die Bekenntnisschriften der lutherischen Kirche*
CA	*Confessio Augustana* (Augsburg Confession)
CS	Common Statement
DS	*Enchiridion Symbolorum*, 36th ed., ed. H. Denzinger and A. Schönmetzer (Freiburg: Herder, 1976)
DV	*Dei Verbum*, Vatican II
ELCA	Evangelical Lutheran Church in America
FC Ep	*Formula of Concord*, Epitome, BC
FC SD	*Formula of Concord*, Solid Declaration, BC
LC	*The Large Catechism*, BC
LG	*Lumen Gentium*, Vatican II
LWF	Lutheran World Federation
LW	*Luther's Works*, Jaroslav Pelikan and Helmut T. Lehmann, general eds. (St. Louis: Concordia Publishing House; and Philadelphia: Fortress; 1[1958]–55[1986])
PG	*Patrologiae cursus completus, Series graeca*, 167 vols. and 2 index vols., ed. J.-P. Migne (Paris: 1857-66, 1928, 1936)
SC	*Sacrosanctum Concilium*, Vatican II
TRE	*Theologische Realenzyklopädie* (Berlin: de Gruyter, 1977–)
UR	*Unitatis Redintegratio*, Vatican II
WA	Martin Luther, *Werke* (Kritische Gesamtausgabe; "Weimarer Ausgabe"; Weimar: Böhlau, 1883–)

Preface

More than a quarter of a century of national-level dialogue between Lutherans and Roman Catholics in the U.S.A. has produced an impressive set of results. Eight volumes of common statements and background documentation have been published; this volume is number nine.

Publication of this text marks a turning point in both the form and the content of Lutheran/Roman Catholic dialogue in the U.S.A. For more than twenty-five years a team of officially appointed theologians has moved from one dialogue topic to another, each following naturally on the one preceding it, all accenting historical, doctrinal questions. During that period of time the ecumenical landscape has changed dramatically, changed in such a way as to require a serious look at where we are in this bilateral relationship and to where it is moving. For this reason a consultation on the future of Lutheran/Roman Catholic relationships in the U.S.A. was held in February of 1993.* Archbishop Rembert G. Weakland, Chairman of

---

* Present at the consultation were the following: Robert W. Bertram, Eugene L. Brand, Edward I. Cassidy, Herbert W. Chilstrom, James R. Crumley Jr., Alan F. Detscher, Karl P. Donfried, Avery Dulles, Gerhard O. Forde, Patrick Granfield, Jeffrey Gros, John F. Hotchkin, Elizabeth A. Johnson, Ralph A. Kempski, Edgar M. Krentz, George Lindbeck, Donald G. Luck, Daniel F. Martensen, Harry McSorley, Harding Meyer, Margaret O'Gara, Ladislas M. Orsy, Duane Priebe, Heinz-Albert Raem, Gail Ramshaw, Thomas P. Rausch, John Reumann, Michael Root, William G. Rusch, Harold C. Skillrud, J. Francis Stafford, Darlis J. Swan, George Tavard, Maxine Washington, Rembert G. Weakland, and Susan K. Wood.

the Committee for Ecumenical and Interreligious Affairs, National Conference of Catholic Bishops, and Bishop Herbert W. Chilstrom of the Evangelical Lutheran Church in America served as chairpersons for the deliberations. Representatives from the U.S.A. dialogue team, the Lutheran World Federation, the Strasbourg Institute for Ecumenical Research, and the Pontifical Council for the Promotion of Christian Unity, as well as bishops, professors, pastors, and priests were among the twenty-eight participants. Recommendations emerging from the consultation included the following:

I. The Lutheran/Roman Catholic dialogue should continue its theological work, however that dialogue may be structured.

II. A future topic for the dialogue should be the understanding and practice of the church as *communio/koinonia*, with a focus on steps required for the realization of full communion between us.

III. A primary task in the coming years should be to develop a synopsis of the U.S.A. dialogue results to date and to establish a process which will lead to a common declaration on justification in the hope that by 1997 it may be possible for the churches to declare that the sixteenth-century condemnations on justification are no longer applicable. This process should also reflect the results of the international and other regional Lutheran/Roman Catholic dialogues.

IV. A greater effort should be made to develop a comprehensive response to, and a common (mutual) reception of, the results of the bilateral dialogue by the members of our churches.

V. A public act or event of affirmation of the goal of full (ecclesial) communion should be made at an appropriate time in the near future.

In June of 1993, the Council of the Lutheran World Federation, meeting in Kristiansand, Norway, saw the need for models to deal adequately with doctrinal issues on the level of the Lutheran communion, this done in coordination with autonomous member churches of the communion. The Council decided that a process to consider lifting the mutual Lutheran-Roman Catholic condemnations of the sixteenth century dealing with justification be established which includes:

1. a sharing with member churches of basic texts and information relating to the recommendation to lift the condemnations,

2. a request for all member churches to study and comment on the specific proposal to lift the condemnations on justification (with

the possibility for appropriate consultation), in order to shape a consensus to be declared by a Lutheran World Federation Assembly, and

3. a commitment (a) to see the Lutheran World Federation Assembly as the summarizer of this process and as the place for a culminating affirmation and (b) to pursue this process in the closest possible collaboration with the Roman Catholic Church.

A Lutheran/Roman Catholic Coordinating Committee has now been established in the United States. Its responsibilities are to implement the recommendations emerging from the U.S.A. consultation that are affirmed by the respective churches, including the formation of a new bilateral dialogue team.

It is the intention of both the Evangelical Lutheran Church in America and the National Conference of Catholic Bishops in the U.S.A. to build upon the remarkable achievements of the past twenty-seven years of Lutheran/Roman Catholic dialogue here in the U.S.A. and upon the accomplishments of the quarter-of-a-century-old international dialogue sponsored by the Roman Catholic Church and the Lutheran World Federation.

On behalf of all the members of this dialogue, we wish to express to the sponsoring churches our deep appreciation for the privilege of our involvement in this significant work for the promotion of the unity of Christ's church.

Co-chairmen:

HAROLD C. SKILLRUD
Bishop of the Southeastern Synod

✠ J. FRANCIS STAFFORD
Archbishop of Denver

COMMON
STATEMENT

THE WORD OF GOD:
SCRIPTURE AND TRADITION

Introduction

1. In 1990 Lutherans and Roman Catholics in this dialogue adopted a statement on questions relating to teachings and practices in regard to Christ, The One Mediator, the Saints, and Mary.[1] Now we have decided to return to a problem that was repeatedly raised since the earliest stage of our ecumenical discussions. In 1965 the first formal meeting focused on the Status of the Nicene Creed as Dogma of the Church. A summary statement issued at the end of the meeting called for further dialogue on two topics:

> Different understandings of the movement from kerygma to dogma obtain in the two communities. Full inquiry must therefore be made into two topics: first, the nature and structure of the teaching authority of the Church; and secondly, the role of Scripture in relation to the teaching office of the Church.[2]

2. The question of teaching authority was eventually treated at length, resulting in three joint statements dealing with Ministry, with Papal Primacy, and with Teaching Authority and Infallibility.[3] Meanwhile, problems relating to the authority and use of Scripture and to the value of tradition surfaced several times in discussion. Yet they were not examined formally, in part because a widespread debate on these matters was in progress in the Christian world in general and in Catholic theology in particular before, during, and after Vatican Council II.[4]

3. Previous joint statements did touch on the question of Scripture and tradition, frequently connecting them with the gospel. In 1967 the statement on the Eucharist as Sacrifice and on the presence of Christ in the Lord's Supper explored the role of Scripture and acknowledged the value of doctrinal traditions, admitting at the same time that "no single vocabulary or conceptual framework can be adequate."[5] In 1970 the statement on the ministry of the people of God and the special ministry of the ordained spoke of the common task "to assimilate valuable elements from different ages and cultures without losing [the] authentic apostolic character [of ministry]."[6] In 1974 the statement on papal primacy reflected extensive work on Scripture and tradition, recognizing that the traditions should be understood and applied in such a way that papal primacy will "serve the gospel and that its exercise of power not subvert Christian freedom."[7] In 1978 the statement on Teaching Authority pointed to Scripture, tradition, and teaching authority as the means by which "the Spirit enables the believing community to settle disputes about the gospel."[8] Yet "whatever infallibility is ascribed to Scripture, the Church, or the pope, it is wholly dependent on the power of God's Word in the gospel."[9] In 1985 the statement on Justification by Faith confessed what Catholic and Lutheran ancestors tried to affirm: they were "willing to be judged by [the gospel] in all our thoughts and actions, our philosophies and projects, our theologies and religious practices."[10] In 1990 Lutherans and Catholics concluded a dialogue on the One Mediator, the Saints, and Mary; they were aware of the controverted question of Scripture and tradition, "the need to investigate biblical extension and magisterial tradition."[11]

4. Since the question of the relationship between Scripture and tradition has always been a component of this dialogue, the Lutheran and Catholic partners in the dialogue judged that it was time to proceed to the investigation that had been foreseen in 1965. In the present exploration of the authority and use of Scripture and tradition, we shall consider first the Lutheran and Catholic views of the Word of God (I). Then we shall take up the relations between Scripture and tradition as the means by which the Word of God is communicated (II). Next we shall turn to the question of the relationship between Jesus Christ, the incarnate Word, and Scripture (III). Finally, we shall address the question of how the Word of God is effective in the community of faith, the church, with special attention to the value of non-apostolic creedal and confessional statements and to the teaching office of the church (IV). In the conclusion we shall summarize

our convergences and divergences (V). The problem of the relationship between Scripture and tradition has had a difficult history in our churches. We hope that the way we address this problem can move our churches beyond the historic opposition between a Lutheran insistence on "Scripture alone" (*sola scriptura*) and a Catholic two-source theory of revelation by Scripture *and* tradition.

I. The Word of God

5. Among Lutherans and Catholics as among other Christians who confess faith in the Triune God, the Word of God is often identified in three ways. The Word of God is, above all, the eternal Son of God who became incarnate as Jesus Christ by the power of the Holy Spirit. As the incarnate Son of God, crucified and risen, Jesus Christ reconciles the fallen world with God, revealing the salvation of humankind and the advent of a new creation.[12]

6. The Word of God is also God's message to humankind, proclaimed as judgment and mercy. Beginning with the Word in creation and continuing in the calling of Israel, the Word of God culminates in the person and work of Jesus Christ, attested through the ages by the power of the Holy Spirit.[13]

7. Furthermore, the Word of God, witnessed through the ages by the power of the Holy Spirit, is a written word, the Holy Scripture. The written word of God is inspired by God's Spirit, who communicates through its authors God's revelation centered in all its fullness in Christ.[14]

8. Scriptures of Israel were accepted as Holy Scripture by Jesus and his disciples and were read by his followers in the light of him. Christ in turn was understood in the light of the Old Testament. Viewing him as the fulfillment of the law and the prophets, the apostolic

church gave a particular interpretation both to Jesus Christ and to the Old Testament.

9. Certain writings of the apostolic church became the authoritative form of the Word of God for the community of faith and were called the New Testament. Both Testaments together constitute the Word of God in written form and are normative for the church.[15]

10. Through that Word, carried by the living tradition, God continues to address the faithful today. The gospel, the good news of salvation through the life, death, and resurrection of Christ, is presented in the inspired Scriptures and formulated in many ways in the church's tradition. The gospel is communicated in word and sacrament; believers who receive it with love and gratitude bear testimony to the gospel in word and deed.

II. Evolution of the Problem

11. Tradition (*paradosis, traditio*), taken in its elementary sense as the act of transmitting the divine message from person to person, is present from the beginning of Israel and of the Christian movement: the message is transmitted from Abraham and Moses to the people of Israel and from Jesus to the disciples; from the disciples to all later believers; from leaders of the communities (*presbyteroi/episcopoi, diaconoi*) to members and catechumens; from parents to children; mutually among believers.[16] At the heart of what is transmitted is the good news of what God has done in the life, death, and resurrection of Jesus Christ.

12. In the early Christian centuries what was transmitted included the following elements:

(1) the Old Testament, which proclaims God's word and deeds in the history of Israel and which for Christians testifies in advance to Jesus as the one in whom God speaks to all of humanity;

(2) the community's memory of Jesus, communicated in the apostolic preaching;

(3) the texts in which the communities of the first centuries recognize their memory of Jesus, together with writings setting forth apostolic teaching, both received as inspired Scriptures (the New Testament);

(4) the actions on which the common life and worship of the believers are focused, inasmuch as they are identified as directly originating in Jesus' own words and deeds (Baptism, Eucharist);

(5) teachings, disciplines, and creedal formulations, in which the early church continued the biblical practice of rejecting false prophets and affirmed the mystery of the faith;

(6) ecclesiastical structures and offices;

(7) artistic expressions and liturgical practices.

13. In the course of centuries the church's life and structure became more elaborate. Traditions extended the original meaning of Scripture by theological interpretation, reformulation, and reconceptualization, often under the influence of other religions and current philosophical thinking.[17] The question of tradition was faced already in the second and third centuries when the Gnostics claimed to have received secret traditions from the apostles. Which traditions were to be accepted? Varying degrees of authority were ascribed to words and decisions formulated by prominent leaders, prophets, and teachers, especially when they met in synods or councils. Once conciliar decisions had multiplied, distinctions were commonly made between earlier and later traditions. An earlier tradition, furthermore, could be discerned at different stages of growth, for instance as witnessed to in the New Testament, or in the writings of the church fathers, or in the ecumenical councils of the patristic period.

14. In the Middle Ages theologians held that all Christian faith is based on Scripture, but this basis was variously interpreted. Thomas Aquinas asserted that even though Scripture has both a literal and a threefold spiritual sense,

> holy Scripture sets up no confusion, since all meanings are based on one, namely the literal sense. From this alone can arguments be drawn, and not . . . from the things said by allegory. Nor does this undo the effect of holy Scripture, for nothing necessary for faith is contained under the spiritual sense that is not openly conveyed through the literal sense elsewhere.[18]

Following him Thomists inferred that only the literal sense of Scripture, as distinct from spiritual senses, can provide conclusive arguments in theological discussion. But it was also held, especially among Nominalists, that Catholic truths include many points of doctrine and practice that, although not literally in Scripture, are deduced from it or are taught by legitimate authority in the church.[19] Such authority was commonly attributed to the early Christian and medieval councils and to the bishop of Rome, believed to be the successor of Peter, whose primacy among the apostles was preserved in the pope's primacy among the bishops. Yet there was no generally accepted doctrine on the relationships between Scripture and later traditions or, within these traditions, between the bishops in council and the bishop of Rome. In the fourteenth and fifteenth centuries conciliarism affirmed the supremacy of councils over the bishop of Rome. However, the supremacy of the bishop of Rome over all councils had supporters both in Rome and in other parts of the church.[20]

15. The question of the authority of Scripture and tradition reached a crisis level in the sixteenth century. Martin Luther found himself caught between his conviction that Scripture teaches justification by faith alone (*sola fide*) and the broad condemnation of his teaching by bishops in Germany and by the bishop of Rome, Leo X. In this instance the position of the authoritative spokesmen for the tradition contradicted the Word of God as Luther read it. Between the Word of God and the decisions of church authorities Luther believed he had no choice. Rather than renounce the teaching of Scripture on the most important point, justification by faith, on which the whole of the Christian life depends, he concluded that the tradition in all its aspects must be subordinated to the clear teaching of Scripture: *sola fides*, *sola gratia*, and *solus Christus* are protected and warranted by *sola scriptura*.

16. Justifying faith, for Luther, along with the whole Western exegetical tradition, arises from and depends upon the hearing of the Word of God (*fides ex auditu*). The way in which the Word comes to hearers is through the oral proclamation of law and gospel, commissioned and normed by the Scriptures. The proclamation itself, the living voice of the Gospel (*viva vox evangelii*) in word and sacrament, is, for Luther, the primary way the Word of God is received in the present because it is the way that the incarnate Word himself now comes to believers. The oral proclamation of the gospel is what might, for Lutherans, be called the "traditioning activity," by analogy with what Catholics call the *actus tradendi*, the handing on of the Word in a given context. However, for Lutherans the relation between Scripture and such traditioning activity is viewed in a light different from the Catholic perspective. Scripture is understood not primarily from the point of view of teaching, as a source of doctrinal truth, but as a source and mandate for the continued preaching of the gospel.

Scripture is the Word *from* God to humans which in turn mandates the appropriate speaking of that Word in the present (the Augustinian tradition of *enarratio*).[21] As such, Scripture is the source and norm for the oral proclamation of the Word of God.

17. Questions about Scripture and tradition tend therefore to be answered differently. A basic question for Luther was whether Scripture mediates a clear Word from God to the despairing sinner. Luther, in a series of dramatic images, likened Scripture to a light shining in the darkness, a pure fountain from which the water of life flows, or the center from which all truth radiates.[22] The fundamental assumption, the "first principle," is the conviction that the Word of God is a promise *from* God and that this Word, hence Scripture, is clear.[23] Were one to approach Scripture as words *about* God, as a book of information about the transcendent One (what Luther called the hidden God), one would indeed find incompleteness, not to say considerable apparent contradiction and obscurity. Then the need for additional and authoritative teaching would be evident. Faith, however, is born of the clear Word *from* God, and therefore can only begin from and rest on the premise of clarity.

18. Acknowledgement of such clarity, however, is not simply a matter of course but, following the image, a matter of being "enlightened," i.e., it is the result of the work of the Holy Spirit through the church. The Word comes from without to enlighten within. Luther can therefore speak of a "twofold clarity of Scripture," internal and external,[24] just as he can speak of a twofold obscurity (internal and external).[25] Internally, the Spirit speaks through the Word to convince and comfort the anxious conscience and enable the believer to judge all doctrine and opinion. Thus Luther could say that without the Holy Spirit one understands nothing of the Scriptures.[26] But in the public ministry of the Word, one cannot preach or teach on the basis of claims to possess the Spirit either individually or collectively. Public ministry of the Word can proceed only on the premise of the external clarity of the preached Word itself, i.e., the inherent power of the Word as address from without. Thus in addition to the internal judgment, there is, for Luther, an external judgment which is "chiefly the concern of leaders and preachers of the Word,"[27] i.e., a judgment exercised in the carrying out of the public office itself. The internal and external clarity are reciprocally related. Internal clarity, perceived by faith, finds the Scriptures to be crystal clear externally. Hence the claim is that Scripture is externally clear, and as such is the only sure and certain arbiter in theological matters. All spirits are to be tested

in the presence of the church at the bar of the external clarity of Scripture. It is, in this reading, precisely because Scripture is so crystal clear, not because it is unclear, that the Holy Spirit is needed. Nonbelievers cannot cope with this clarity. The light blinds eyes too long accustomed to the dark. Only as one is in the Spirit who inspired the Scriptures can one see. In the Spirit, that is, one can let the Scriptures stand in their external clarity.

19. The aim of the distinction between internal and external clarity is to avoid subjectivism in the public use of Scripture, particularly in theological argument. One cannot preach, teach, or argue on the basis of claims to possessing the Spirit. On the contrary, the Spirit leads to acceptance of the external clarity of Scripture and its mandates. External clarity does not mean, however, that there are no passages that are difficult to understand. Such difficulties are, however, of an order different from the word of promise from God. They are due to incomplete knowledge or insufficient mastery of linguistic, grammatical, and historical matters. Furthermore, even if the Scriptures are obscure in one place on matters of moment, this obscurity is removed in other places.

20. Clarity comes from being grasped in the Spirit by the promise from and in Christ. Jesus as Messiah, Son of God, and Savior is the essential Word from God, the content and center of the entire Scriptures, both Old and New Testaments (*die Mitte der Schrift*).[28] This in turn entails the fundamental claim that Scripture interprets itself (*sui ipsius interpres*).[29] The root problem in interpreting the Scriptures is the lack of our internal clarity. Scripture cannot, therefore, be treated merely as the object of our interpretive activity. By virtue of its own external clarity, Scripture is understood as a "clear and bright light" that finds, enlightens, judges, and saves those who hear and believe its Word. All the instances of *sola* (*sola scriptura, sola gratia, solus Christus, sola fides*) entail and mutually qualify one other.

21. Luther and the Lutheran Confessions see the question of tradition in the light of this understanding and use of Scripture. *Sola scriptura* does not mean that tradition is rejected *per se*, but rather that Scripture establishes itself as the final arbiter in matters of faith and life, particularly in cases of dispute. Tradition stands under, not over, the scriptural Word and its proclamation. Scripture thus evokes a tradition that accords primacy and ultimacy to Scripture itself. Such an understanding of tradition and the claim that Scripture interprets itself by no means exclude the activity of exegetes and theologians, the use of commentaries, and similar kinds of research. In the light

of this understanding of the traditioning activity, the church is regarded as the community of believers, listening to what the Spirit has to say through the Scriptures. The tradition is an account of what the community has heard. The community is the custodian of this tradition and through it summons subsequent hearers to careful listening.

22. The basic aim of such interpretive activity for Lutherans, however, is not to supplement a supposed insufficiency of Scripture or to clarify its alleged obscurities. Rather it is the attempt to allow the light of Scripture to illumine our darkness, to have the subjectivism of our spirits overcome by the Spirit who speaks through Scripture. Everything in the church's practice, preaching, and teaching is to be subordinate to the Word of Scripture. Both the structure of transmission and the content of what is transmitted must be judged according to the norm of Scripture.

23. But then one may ask: How can Lutherans insist upon *sola scriptura* and at the same time speak as they do of "Scripture and Confessions?" How could the Lutheran Confessors on the one hand "pledge [them]selves to the prophetic and apostolic writings of the Old and New Testaments . . . as the only true norm" when in the same breath they declare their own recent Augsburg Confession to be "a single, universally accepted, certain and common form of doctrine" (*Form der Lehre*) by which all other churchly writings are to be "judged and regulated?"[30] The explanation lies in the Lutheran understanding of *confessio*. The biblical Word shares its unique normativeness with such postbiblical confessions only because and if that is what they are: "con-fession" (literally a "saying with"), *homologia*, a same-saying, a saying-back of that original scriptural Word.

24. In the Lutheran Confessions the biblical Word is pictured as the ever-contemporary "Judge," "the only Judge" (*der einig Richter*) which in each new age calls forth "witnesses" to itself. The "confessions" (another courtroom image) are that judge's witnesses, arraigned before their accusers. The confessions are the *Zeugen* (witnesses) in which, as in the ancient creeds, "the doctrine of the prophets and apostles" is again brought to speech "in post-apostolic times" and "in our times."[31] The confessions are what the *Judge* evokes—not merely agrees or disagrees with after hearing them out, but typically of the courtrooms of that day, what the judge actively prompts the witnesses to testify. The judge is the Word of God and is ultimately that Judge, Jesus Christ, by whom the confessors hope to be vindicated on the last day.[32] Confessions have been called echoes.

They are the scriptural Word of God hearing itself coming back, if always in new historical contexts.

25. Thus the "form of doctrine" which defines the Confessions is not merely like but is the selfsame form which defines Scripture itself. Scripture and confessions are virtually uni-form, their common identity being the one Word of God. True, the confessions' doctrinal authority is not original but altogether derivative. Nevertheless, the authority they do have is a reassertion of Scripture's own authority and is therefore normative for "all other [churchly] writings."[33] In this context where "Scripture and tradition" means Scripture and confession, there are not two magisterial authorities, but one, the biblical Word of God—in this sense, *sola scriptura*.

26. The Catholic response to Lutheranism was given by the Council of Trent (1545–63). But it was given in categories other than those of Luther. At the fourth session (1546) the Council expressed its intention that "the purity of the gospel, purged of all errors, may be preserved in the church." It was this gospel that "Our Lord Jesus Christ, the Son of God, first proclaimed with his own lips" and "then . . . bade it be preached to every creature through his apostles as the source of all saving truth and rule of conduct" (*fontem omnis et salutaris veritatis et morum disciplinae*).[34] The Council fathers then expressed their "perception" that "this truth and this rule are contained in written books and in unwritten traditions that were received by the apostles from the mouth of Christ himself, or have come down to us, handed on as it were from the apostles themselves at the inspiration of the Holy Spirit." In the light of this perception the Council concluded: "Following the example of the orthodox fathers, the Council accepts and venerates with a like feeling of piety and reverence[35] all the books of both the Old and the New Testament, since the one God is the author of both, as well as the traditions concerning both faith and conduct, as either directly spoken by Christ or dictated by the Holy Spirit, which have been preserved in unbroken sequence in the catholic church."[36]

27. In the eyes of later centuries, the Council of Trent left a number of questions unanswered: What are the relations between the gospel as source of all saving truth and the Scriptures and traditions? In what way do the Scriptures and the traditions function as sources of doctrine? If some apostolic traditions were inspired by the Holy Spirit, why restrict such inspiration to the apostolic period? Is the gospel to be found in its entirety in Scripture alone, or is it there only in part? Are the traditions necessary to identify the

gospel? Generally speaking, later Catholic theology was divided between two interpretations of the Tridentine text. Advocates of two sources of faith, Scripture and tradition, were the majority up to the eve of Vatican II. Yet there were also advocates of some Catholic forms of *sola Scriptura*.[37]

28. The controversial situation that followed the Reformation brought something of a shift regarding the problem of Scripture and tradition. At first, Catholics reacted against what they considered to be Luther's subjectivism and against the spread of private interpretations of the Bible. They underlined the need for authoritative interpretation, and they identified the bishops as the authentic interpreters of Scripture. Even though there was a growth in theories of the inspiration of Scripture among Catholic interpreters (as well as among Lutherans), controversy led many Catholics to regard Scripture as insufficient: they affirmed the binding value of complementary traditions received from the apostles. Likewise under the pressure of controversy, some Lutherans understood the *sola scriptura* to exclude tradition. Special theories of inspiration and inerrancy developed to fortify scriptural authority.[38] Though there was no uniform development, there was a general erosion of the original Reformation view which had found its theological uniqueness in the premise of the external clarity and self-interpretation of Scripture. Controversy thus tended to obscure basic issues and to block ecumenical progress. The two sides hardened, at least in popular understanding, into unfortunate, if not impossible alternatives: an "insufficient" or perhaps "obscure" Scripture in need of extra tradition on the one hand, and an isolated and formalized *sola scriptura* on the other.

29. With the dogmatic constitution *Dei Verbum* of Vatican II, convergence between Catholic and Lutheran understandings began to emerge. The Council affirmed that all divine revelation was brought to perfection in Jesus Christ[39] and that the gospel was written down by inspiration.[40] Vatican II also formulated the general Catholic assumption that there cannot be a real contradiction between Scripture and what the church transmits: "Holy Tradition and Holy Scripture form the one sacred deposit of God's Word which has been entrusted to the church." At the same time, Vatican II related Scripture and tradition to the magisterium: "The task of providing an authentic interpretation of God's Word in Scripture or tradition has been entrusted only to the Church's living magisterium . . . ." Yet the magisterium is "not above God's Word, it rather serves the

Word . . . ." It does so in such a way that "holy tradition, holy Scripture and the Church's magisterium are, according to God's wise design, so interconnected and united that none can stand without the others . . . ."[41]

30. Within this functional unity Scripture is the Word of God inasmuch as it is consigned to writing under the inspiration of the Spirit. So great is the power of the Word of God in Scripture that it remains the source and support of the energy, faith, and life of the church. "Accordingly, all the preaching of the church, as indeed the entire Christian religion, should be nourished and ruled by sacred Scripture" (*nutriatur et regatur oportet*).[42] Tradition hands on the Word of God in its full purity through faithful preaching and teaching.[43] Tradition is a function of the Holy Spirit in history:

> What was handed on by the apostles includes everything that contributes to the holiness of life and the increase in faith of the people of God; and so the church, in her teaching, life, and worship, perpetuates and hands on to all generations all that she herself is, all that she believes.[44]

31. In this context preserving the Word of God is the task of the whole Christian people, while the teaching office has a specific ministerial function, teaching only what has been handed on, listening to it devoutly, guarding it scrupulously, and explaining it faithfully, thereby offering an authentic interpretation of it for the sake of salvation.[45] The significance of this relationship of service becomes clearer when it is remembered that the first schema had proposed that the magisterium be considered the proximate norm of the truth (*proxima veritatis norma*) of revelation. This formulation seemed to suggest that Scripture and tradition were only remote norms, to be ascertained through the magisterium. In the final text, however, the magisterium is described not as an institution for discovering new truth but as an office of pastoral service to the life of the apostolic Christian community, formed by the Word of God. On balance, Scripture, tradition, and teaching office are distinct but interrelated elements that contribute to the communication of God's saving grace in Christ.

III. Theological Considerations

32. In the wake of Vatican II the question between Lutherans and Catholics amounts to this: Is the permanent interconnection between Scripture, tradition, and magisterium that is envisaged in Catholic thought compatible with the historic Lutheran principle that Scripture alone provides the norm by which tradition and magisterium are to be judged? Because the standard formulations that are commonly used by Lutherans and by Catholics are obviously different, the theological question may also be framed this way: Are there conditions under which the two positions may be reconciled? What follows is a delineation of Lutheran and Catholic views on Scripture and tradition so that points of convergence can be discerned.

33. Because Lutherans ascribe prime importance to the oral proclamation of the Word of God, the *sola scriptura* principle not only does not rule out but demands continuing interpretation and application of Scripture. In addition, the Lutheran Confessions recognize the authority of the patristic tradition and early councils. Summing up the doctrines it has presented, for example, the Augsburg Confession argues that its position is in continuity with the writings of the ancient church: "Since this teaching is grounded clearly on the Holy Scriptures and is not contrary or opposed to that of the universal Christian church, or even of the Roman church (in so far as the latter's teaching is reflected in the writings of the Fathers), we think

that our opponents cannot disagree with us in the articles set forth above."[46] Similarly, in the Apology the Confessors responded to the charge that they had undermined the authority of bishops by attesting to their "deep desire to maintain church polity and various ranks of the ecclesiastical hierarchy, although they were created by human authority," because "the Fathers had good and useful reasons for instituting ecclesiastical discipline in the manner described by the ancient canons."[47] Stressing the conviction that "our confession is true, godly, and catholic," the Apology declares the importance of right governance and affirms the office of those who teach the Word of God and administer the sacraments: "We want at this time to declare our willingness to keep the ecclesiastical and canonical polity."[48] There is one condition: that bishops cease condemning the sort of doctrine that Lutherans confess and allow the preaching of the gospel that is right and true. Thus it is characteristic of the Lutheran position to affirm the function of the episcopal teaching office if it exercises its basic responsibility to promote trustworthy preaching of the abundant mercy of God poured out in Jesus Christ apart from any merits of sinners.

34. Both the Lutheran Confessions and the Council of Trent spoke only of traditions in the plural. Now, however, the distinction between tradition and traditions is widely used in theology and can be described in this way. Tradition involves a process in a community; in this case, it refers to the Word of God precisely as it is handed on in the church: *verbum Dei traditum*. Tradition also denotes the content of what is handed on, namely, the totality of the gracious presence of Christ passed on in history through the power of the Spirit in the life, teaching, and worship of the church. Insofar as the community is the locus of Christ's redeeming presence in the world, tradition connotes that the church hands on in a living way all that it is, all that it believes.[49] Traditions (*traditiones*) are particular ideas, formulations, and practices handed down in this process. To some of these the church commits itself as true expressions of the gospel, for example, *homoousios* and infant baptism. Others become customary in the course of the church's life, many of them not essential to the preaching of the gospel but valuable for Christian life. It is also possible for unsound customs or superstitious beliefs to creep into common use, so that discernment is needed to judge which traditions do not compromise the gospel and which are distortions.

35. In examining the question of what status may be given to human traditions in the church, the Apology of the Augsburg

Confession teaches "that we receive forgiveness of sins freely for Christ's sake by faith"[50] and that this must be kept paramount in the church. Hence one should resist traditions that compromise the gospel; that is, traditions that are promoted as if they merit the forgiveness of sin, or are acts of worship that please God as righteousness, or are performed of necessity because their omission is judged to be a sin. Yet even the apostles ordained many things, legitimate traditions that preserved order for the sake of peace, "and they did not set them down as though they could not be changed."[51] Hence, "This is the simple way to interpret traditions. We should know that they are not necessary acts of worship, and yet we should observe them in their place and without superstition, in order to avoid offenses."[52] Thus it is characteristic of the Lutheran position to allow for traditions that do not compromise the gospel and to cherish those that effectively promote it, even though these are not mentioned in Scripture.

36. In this perspective the *sola* of *sola scriptura*, as it is intended in the Lutheran Confessions, is not a term that would rule out the usefulness of everything that is not stated in the Scriptures. Like the other instances of *sola*, it expresses all that is necessary for the proper reception of divine saving grace, fundamentally pointing to Christ alone. The bright and shining light that is Scripture is the norm or rule that ensures adherence to the gospel in the historical proliferation of human traditions in the church. As the written testimony of all that Christ is and does for the sake of our salvation, it needs no supplement. Rather, Scripture alone is the arbiter in matters of faith and life.

37. The affirmation that *sola scriptura* as source and norm does not exclude the function of a teaching office or the value of many traditions in the church is, at first glance, a negative statement. However, there is a positive Lutheran investment in the formula, particularly with regard to the clarity (*claritas*) and self-interpretation (*sui ipsius interpres*) of Scripture, and its material sufficiency. Scripture in itself, as the clear, written Word of God, gives the assurance that we are saved by grace through faith in Christ alone rather than through any works or merits of our own.

38. In the sixteenth century these considerations were a key area of polemic. Lutherans, on the one hand, held that the written word of God witnesses to all that needs to be known about the salvation of sinners and testifies to this so brilliantly that the general reader, the ordinary baptized person, can grasp the good news. The certainty of

faith is based on the word of the gospel proclaimed according to Scripture alone. Catholics, on the other hand, asserted at that time that Scripture on its own is neither sufficient nor clear, thus making necessary the writings of the fathers and interpretation by the community.[53] This position was nuanced insofar as the Council of Trent retained as binding only apostolic traditions, written and unwritten, with even these having no permanent value unless they dealt with matters of faith and morals. Although this approach converged with statements of the Lutheran Confessions on apostolic tradition, it differed from the *sola scriptura* understood by Lutherans.

39. Furthermore, Catholics at that time argued that *sola scriptura* was largely responsible for the theoretical and practical excesses of various sectarian groups labelled enthusiasts (*Schwärmer*) by Luther. These enthusiasts affirmed the right of all believers to private interpretations of the Bible, rejected the value of all traditions, denied the existence of any authority able to speak for the church, and consequently destroyed the received ecclesial structure. While this radical critique was aimed at Lutherans and Catholics alike, it seemed to Catholics to be a consequence of disconnecting Scripture from traditions and the teaching office, and thus Luther's *sola scriptura* was blamed for the spread of such ideas.

40. Today the issue assumes a somewhat different shape. For Lutherans *solus Christus* radically entails *sola gratia*, *sola fides*, and *sola scriptura*, all of which must be taken together as part of an integrated whole that proclaims how persons come to the salvation that God has appointed for them: only Scripture can make clear that it is Christ alone, by grace, through faith, who saves sinners. There is a lively suspicion on the Lutheran side that the Catholic appeal to tradition and the teaching office erodes and subverts this teaching of justification by grace and faith alone. If Scripture must be supplemented by something else, if its word of truth is so ambiguous that it needs interpretation by a normative authority, then its nature as the clear and bright written Word of God is compromised, with devastating effects on the power of the gospel to assure people of Christ's effective saving action.

41. Convergence, however, is opened up by Vatican II's position on Scripture, tradition, and the teaching office, a position not won without keen struggle and lively debate. The first schema on the topic, which was rejected, had urged recognition that tradition had material content to offer over and above what was contained in Scripture. (This is the neo-scholastic two-source theory.) The final teaching sees

them more as a functioning unity, with Scripture having a nourishing and ruling function while tradition interprets and hands on the whole living experience of Christ testified to by Scripture. Underlying this shift are two basic ideas, namely, that tradition is a Spirit-inspired process in the church rather than a set of materials, and that it is concerned with the life of the community in all of its dimensions, including personal example, prayer and worship, and structures, rather than with teachings only.

42. The standard Catholic teaching now holds that both Scripture and tradition derive from the same wellspring who is Christ, the source of grace and truth. Christ is witnessed to by his followers, who through their oral preaching, example, and institutions handed on what they had received. They committed the message of salvation to writing, giving us the Word of God in Scripture. Whether written in Scripture or preached and lived, the saving power and presence of Christ continues in the living voice of the gospel heard in the church through the ages.

43. Both the vigor of the conciliar debate and subsequent developments show that the Catholic community is in a process of rethinking that is not yet finished. It has clearly moved to reaffirm the irreplaceable centrality of Scripture for the preaching, teaching, and life of the church. It has moved away from the two-source theory of revelation which ascribed independent validity to tradition as a separate source of faith. At the same time it has not explicitly affirmed *sola scriptura* in at least two important Lutheran senses.

44. *Clarity.* The standard Catholic position is not that Scripture is unclear. To the contrary, it is lucidly articulate about God's saving will and, in the New Testament, about how this becomes living and effective in Christ for those who believe. It has the power so to interpret itself to the receptive reader. But for Catholics Scripture is the book of the church, its new writings written and received by the apostolic church which also interpreted the Scriptures of Israel in the light of Christ. Hence Scripture would be less than perfectly clear if it were read in isolation from the community, its tradition, and its interpretation. For Catholics to say this is not to compromise the certainty of faith but to broaden the base from which it is derived.[54]

45. *Norm or rule of faith.* In the Catholic view Scripture, tradition, and teaching office are so linked and joined together that one cannot stand without the others.[55] However, the criterion or critical principle to be used to judge distortions that historically creep in has not been clearly articulated. Scripture is affirmed as a rule that governs

39

preaching and the whole of religion, but it is not affirmed as the only rule.[56] During the conciliar debate this lack of a clear criterion was noted, along with the fact that there are distorting as well as legitimate traditions. As a result, while saying that the church hands on all that she is, all that she believes, the Council deleted the phrase *"omne quod habet,"* all that she has, realizing that not all the church has is always and everywhere in accord with the gospel.[57] Nevertheless, the Council did not endorse Scripture as the sole rule of faith, thus leaving unresolved questions about the necessity of criticism of tradition and the teaching office, and about the critical principle to be followed in conflict.[58]

46. Is there a possibility of convergence between Lutheran and Catholic theological positions on Scripture and tradition? A measure of agreement already exists. Lutherans adhere to apostolic and patristic tradition in the form of creeds, christological and trinitarian doctrines, church order, and the like, insofar as these are normed by Scripture, and they allow for developments in history such as the Lutheran Confessions according to the same rule. They attach great importance to oral proclamation and affirm the legitimacy of episcopal authority and the permissibility of human traditions. Catholics, by contrast, affirm the centrality of Scripture as the word of God for the life of the church. They have a growing appreciation of its normative character as it nourishes and rules preaching and the whole of religion. They no longer speak of tradition as a separate source of revelation. While affirming that there is growth in the understanding of the realities and the words which have been handed down, they see tradition as fundamentally this handing on and thus as a process of transmitting something already given.

47. There is obviously convergence here, although not complete unity. Both communities wholeheartedly affirm *solus Christus*: we are saved through faith in Jesus Christ alone. On the question of *sola scriptura*, basic theological affirmations can be made in common while there are still differences regarding Scripture's relation to tradition in the life of the church.

IV. The Living Word in the Community of Faith

48. The church in every age and in every part of the world continues to preach and receive the Word of God in faith and to respond actively in word and deed. Through its proclamation and response the church echoes the Word of God communicated through Scripture and earlier tradition, and makes it possible for believers everywhere to have access to the Word of God, no matter how far removed they may be in time, place, and culture from the original events of revelation. Through the power of the Holy Spirit the Word of God lives on in the memory of the church and is differently interpreted in different contexts.

49. Lutherans and Catholics are at one in their conviction that the Bible has a preeminent and irreplaceable role as the inspired Word of God committed to writing once for all. The Bible sustains and strengthens the faith of its readers and becomes for them an abiding source and guide for life in Christ.[59] The Word of God as permanently given in Scripture is to be proclaimed in and by the church, the community of faith.

50. When the church assembles for worship, as it regularly does on Sundays, the Word of God is transmitted through proclamation and sacrament. A qualified minister is appointed to preside at the service. The readings at the liturgy and many of the prayers are taken from Holy Scripture, which accordingly plays a paramount role in the worship of the church.[60] The sermon commonly takes the form of

41

proclamation based on biblical texts or that of exposition of a Scripture lesson, especially the Gospel for the day, and these are the forms of preaching most strongly encouraged by both our churches.[61] Not only preaching, but all forms of catechesis and religious instruction, not to say theology itself, are based primarily upon the Word of God in Scripture.[62]

51. The Word of God is not to be understood as an inert collection of words to be extracted from Scripture as stones from a quarry. It is living and active, the demanding voice of the law and the promising voice of the gospel (Jer 23:29; Heb 4:12). God is present in the Word, accomplishing the divine purpose (Is 55:11), ending the old and bringing in the new, exposing sin and working salvation in those who believe (Rom 1:16). This view of the relationship between Scripture and the proclaimed Word is deeply rooted in the Lutheran confessional tradition and is consonant with Catholic teaching.[63]

52. The role of liturgy in the shaping and testing of doctrine deserves fuller exploration than has yet been given to it by Lutherans and Catholics in dialogue. A convergence on the subject is noted in an earlier volume.[64] Because faith is continually renewed by personal confrontation with the realities of faith in communal prayer and sacramental worship, the church has from ancient times recognized the intimate connection between liturgy and belief, between the *lex orandi* and the *lex credendi*.[65] In both our traditions the axiom *lex orandi–lex credendi* is cited, but there are different views regarding the relative priorities. Expressing a more recent Catholic view, Pius XII pointed out that liturgical prayer offers testimonies and assists in the determination of doctrine, but he added that, "if one desires to differentiate and describe the relationship between faith and the sacred liturgy in absolute and general terms," the rule of belief should determine the rule of prayer.[66] From a Lutheran point of view, there is an interaction of prayer, testimony, and doctrine in the life of the church.[67] Recognizing the power of the liturgy to shape belief, Luther, like the other Reformers of his age, set out to revise the ceremonies to bring them into conformity with the Word of God.[68] Notwithstanding their different emphases, Lutherans and Catholics agree in principle that sometimes the liturgy must be revised in order to make it a more faithful instrument for communicating the Word of God, while at other times the explicit teaching of the church may be enriched and improved by reflection on the implications of the forms of prayer and worship.

53. The Word of God is transmitted also by means of the confession of faith in word and deed. Scripture reports how the Israelites, in a pagan environment, and sometimes in the face of persecution, confessed their faith in the one true God who had saved them from slavery. The New Testament tells the story of how the apostles and their companions spread the good news of Christ through their courageous witness, extending at times to martyrdom. Embedded in the New Testament are brief confessional formulas in which Christians articulated their distinctive identity, proclaiming their faith in the one God and in Jesus as sole Lord, against opposing views, often polytheistic (1 Cor 8:5–6; Eph 4:5; cf. Rom 10:9). These confessional statements have inspired modern "confessions of faith," especially in situations of crisis.[69] Recently the Lutheran World Federation, considering that such a crisis had arisen in Southern Africa, issued a statement that suspended membership of churches that tolerated apartheid.[70] Vatican Council II, in its Decree on Ecumenism, exhorted all Christians to "confess together before the whole world their faith in the triune God and in the incarnate Son of God, our Redeemer and Lord."[71] This decree expressed appreciation for "those Christians who openly confess Jesus Christ as God and Lord and as the sole Mediator between God and man" and who feel compelled to "bear witness to their faith among all the peoples of the earth."[72]

54. Although confessions of faith grounded in our common Scriptures can serve as a bond between our traditions, we still have to deal with a heritage of mutually opposing confessional statements. The Augsburg Confession of 1530 expressed ecumenical reform proposals on the part of the Lutheran party, but it has never been formally accepted by Catholic ecclesiastical authorities. Nevertheless Pope John Paul II in 1980 recognized that this confession reflects "a full accord on fundamental and central truths."[73] Some later Lutheran confessional writings, such as the Smalcald Articles, were directed in part against what were perceived as Roman Catholic errors. Similarly, from the Catholic side, the Profession of Faith of Pius IV (1564) was intended as a warning against what were perceived as false doctrines of the Protestant Reformers. A major concern of twentieth-century ecumenical dialogues has been to bridge the gap that is evident in these polemical confessions.[74]

55. Together with Scripture, a resource for overcoming the divisions has been, and still is, the adherence of our respective churches to three early Christian creeds, the Apostles' Creed, the

Nicene-Constantinopolitan Creed, and the Athanasian Creed.[75] We agree that the Nicene dogma of the *homoousios* successfully "gathered up the sense of the Scriptures," to borrow the expression of Athanasius,[76] and to that extent expresses the Word of God. Catholics may speak of these creeds, as do the Lutheran authors of the Formula of Concord, as being "catholic and general creeds possessed of the highest authority" (*illa catholica et generalia summa auctoritatis symbola*).[77]

56. Like the creeds, the solemn definitions and anathemas of early councils, such as Nicaea, Constantinople, Ephesus, and Chalcedon, are accepted in our respective churches as authoritative statements of the apostolic faith. Some differences, however, remain. Lutherans avoid speaking of infallible decisions, but they can agree with Catholics that the dogma of Nicaea about God the Son, for example, is a "definitive reply to an ever-recurring question."[78] Catholics, while holding that such determinations of the faith are irreversible, can agree with Lutherans that the language and conceptuality of the early councils must not be absolutized.[79] The formulations of dogma are subject to human and historical limitations;[80] they demand new interpretations as new questions arise and as older cultural limitations are overcome. In the interpretation and reformulation of dogma the testimony of the Scriptures must always be fundamental,[81] but there can be normative doctrinal developments beyond the express statement of Scripture.

57. An example in both our traditions may be found in the endorsement of the title *Theotokos*, "God-bearer" or "Mother of God," for Mary.[82] While the title had apparently been coined earlier, the Council of Ephesus (431) adopted it as a corollary of the affirmation that Jesus Christ, while being both human and divine, was a single, undivided being. The christological synthesis of Jesus as God and man fostered the conviction that it was possible, and indeed necessary, to give Mary the title of *Theotokos* inasmuch as she gave birth to the divine Son according to his human nature. This development of ancient theology, formulated in terms of Greek culture, found general acceptance in most churches of the East as well as in the West. They all agreed that the dogmatic statement needed to be made authoritatively for the purpose of explicating and safeguarding a basic point of faith found in Scripture.

58. An example of development of Marian doctrine not shared by both our traditions is the Assumption of the Blessed Virgin Mary. On November 1, 1950, Pope Pius XII solemnly declared the bodily

Assumption of Mary into heaven to be a dogma of Catholic faith. The first written evidence of a belief in the Assumption goes back to the apocryphal literature on the "Dormition of the Virgin" which appeared in the late fourth century. While the Assumption was widely accepted in the West from the Middle Ages on, it is a doctrine found neither in the New Testament nor in the early fathers. The papal bull *Munificentissimus Deus* itself admitted that ". . . theologians and preachers have [often] . . . been rather free in their use of events and expressions taken from Sacred Scripture to explain their belief in the Assumption" (26).[83] Such scriptural usage, indeed, was often no more than an accommodation of unrelated texts by allegory or spiritual intuition. The document also invoked the liturgy but pointed out that liturgy "does not engender Catholic faith but springs from it" (20). Liturgy, in this case, is a witness, not a source. Thus the decisive element in the definition of the dogma appears to be the universal assent of the episcopate supported by, and perhaps based on, the faith of the people. These elements are combined with the view that such a belief, having long been accepted and being universally held by Catholics as divinely revealed, is capable of being declared a dogma by the supreme teaching authority of the church (41).

59. Although Lutherans have insisted that necessary articles of faith must be grounded in Scripture, they have not rejected all postbiblical formulations. A few spoke of a "patristic consensus" (*consensus patrum*) or a "consensus of the first five centuries" (*consensus quinquesaecularis*)[84] in order to express their sense of solidarity with the church catholic and their concern for the proper expression of biblical truth. When Socinians threatened the trinitarian basis of the church's confession on the ground that the doctrine of the Trinity was not literally in Scripture, Lutheran theologians rejected the notion that all true doctrine had to be simply and literally present in the Bible.[85] Nevertheless, Lutherans are critical of other postbiblical formulations. While they agree that as a matter of historical fact Marian devotion in the fourth century contributed to the definition of the *Theotokos* title, they cannot see how such devotion provides a legitimate basis for the dogma of Mary's Assumption into heaven. Here the earlier move from biblical text to postbiblical formulation to designate Mary as *Theotokos*, which extols Christ, has not been simply replicated; rather, interpretation has been stretched beyond what Lutherans consider to be a legitimate use of Scripture. For them, therefore, a dogmatic declaration such as that of 1950 cannot be justified.[86]

60. In both the Lutheran and the Catholic traditions, great importance is attached to the process of assuring sound doctrine. The structures for authenticating doctrine, however, are not the same.[87] According to Catholic doctrine the college of bishops, together with the pope as its head, succeeding respectively to the college of the apostles and to Peter, received from Christ the duty of teaching the faith with divine authority. Assisted by the Holy Spirit, these officeholders can on occasion make irrevocable determinations of the faith, binding on the whole church.[88] Such decisions, while they embody or protect the Word of God, are not regarded as being themselves the Word of God. They depend upon God's Word given in Scripture and tradition.

61. According to the Augsburg Confession the bishop is a pastor exercising the function of oversight and thus possesses the "power of the keys" to teach and preach the Word of God and to condemn doctrine that is contrary to the gospel.[89] In the Lutheran churches represented in this dialogue the highest teaching authority is exercised by the churchwide assembly. The differing attitudes of Lutherans and Catholics toward episcopacy, papacy, and infallible teaching authority have been explored in volumes 4, 5, and 6 of this dialogue.

62. The Word of God is efficacious when it is received and welcomed by the faithful. Lutherans and Catholics alike hold that in accepting the faith as set forth in Scripture, creeds, and confessions members of the church submit their minds and hearts to the Word of God, and this reception, they add, is a vital, personal response empowered by the Holy Spirit who testifies within the hearts of the faithful.[90] Catholics understand that the teaching of popes and bishops, while it is authenticated by the Word of God and the authority of these teachers, is differently nuanced and sometimes takes on a richer significance in proportion to the spiritual gifts and talents of those who receive it.[91] When consensus is achieved between the authoritative teachers and the faithful, this unanimity is considered by Catholics to be a sign of the working of the Holy Spirit, who leads the whole church into the truth of revelation.[92]

63. Vatican II spoke in this connection of the "sense of the faith" (*sensus fidei*), and many theologians, especially in the Catholic tradition, have referred to the concordant sense (or consent) of the faithful (*sensus fidelium*) as a criterion of true doctrine. These terms, infrequently used in Lutheranism, can have a positive meaning in both our traditions, but must be cautiously applied. Catholic theologians, like Lutheran theologians, are generally aware of the danger

of confusing the "sense of the faithful" with public opinion. Public opinion, even in the church, is not a norm of doctrine; it is ambiguous to the extent that it is influenced by sinful or merely worldly considerations and lacks solid grounding in Scripture and apostolic tradition. The "sense of the faithful," as an authentic response to the Word of God, cannot be verified in a merely statistical way, but must be identified as a discernment issuing from a genuine obedience of faith.[93]

V. Conclusion

64. Our discussions have shown a large measure of agreement and some remaining differences of doctrine or emphasis. We note these significant points of agreement:

• Holy Scripture has preeminent status as the Word of God, committed to writing in an unalterable manner.

• Before the Old and New Testaments existed in written form, the Word of God was carried by tradition.

• Under the guidance of the Holy Spirit Scripture gives rise to the oral proclamation of law and gospel.

• The preeminent status of Scripture does not exclude the function of a teaching office or the legitimacy of doctrinal traditions that protect and promote the reliance of the faithful on the gospel message of Christ and grace alone (*solus Christus* and *sola gratia*).

• There are no historically verifiable apostolic traditions that are not attested in some way by Scripture.

• Not all true doctrine needs to be simply and literally present in the Bible, but may be deduced from it.

• The teaching of doctrine in the church is never above the Word of God, but must serve that Word and be in conformity with it.

65. We note these principal differences:

• Lutherans hold that Scripture alone is the ultimate norm by which traditions must be judged. Catholics hold that the decisive norm by which doctrines or traditions are judged is Scripture together with living apostolic tradition, which is perpetuated in the church through the influence of the Holy Spirit.

• Lutherans "question the appropriateness of speaking of the church's teaching office as infallible."[94] They consequently hold that all magisterial decisions are in principle subject to revision and correction in the light of a better reading of Scripture. Catholics hold that under certain conditions the bishop of Rome or the college of bishops with him, thanks to the assistance of the Holy Spirit, speak with infallibility. The gift of infallibility does not preclude further refinement in the teaching but gives assurance that the teaching will not have to be reversed.

• As a consequence of the two differences just noted, Lutherans and Catholics differ in their understandings of the development of doctrine. Lutherans recognize some developments, notably those declared by the early ecumenical councils, as expressing the true meaning of Scripture, but they do not accept developments that lack what Lutherans perceive as a clear basis in Scripture. For Catholics the supreme teaching authority of the church, with the assistance of the Holy Spirit, can proclaim doctrines expressing the faith of the whole church that go beyond the explicit statements of Scripture and beyond what can be strictly deduced from these statements.

66. In the present round of dialogue we have found that the Lutheran *sola scriptura*, when taken in conjunction with other Reformation principles, such as *sola fide*, *sola gratia*, and *solus Christus*, gives rise to a dynamic understanding of the Word of God that approximates what Catholics often understand as tradition in the active sense: the Spirit-assisted "handing on" of God's revelation in Christ. We also found that Catholics no longer speak of tradition as a separate source but see it, together with Scripture, as the Word of God for the life of the church. Scripture is seen as central to the preaching of the church and as the very soul of theology. For Lutherans and Catholics alike the gospel is God's free and undeserved gift in Christ, the only Mediator, presented in the Scriptures that were inspired by the Spirit, proposed and explained by the preaching of the apostles and of the church's ministers, witnessed to in the church's creeds and confessions, formulated in many ways in the church's tradition, offered to believers in the celebration of Word and sacrament, received in faith with love and gratitude, and attested in the lives and

utterances of the saints. Thus the present statement ties together the previous work of this dialogue in a joint affirmation of the one faith in Christ alone that is communicated fundamentally and abidingly in Holy Scripture, the written form of the Word of God.

Notes

1. L/RC 8.
2. L/RC 1, p. 32.
3. L/RC 4; 5; 6.
4. There is abundant literature; e.g., Oscar Cullmann, *La Tradition* (Neuchâtel: Delachaux et Niestlé, 1953); Ellen Flesseman-van Leer, *Tradition and Scripture in the Early Church* (Assen: Van Gorcum, 1954). This subject was the object of statements by the Consultation on Church Union ("Scripture, Tradition and the Guardians of Tradition" [Oberlin, 1963] in *COCU: The Reports of the Four Meetings* [Cincinnati: Forward Movement Publications, 1963], 23–32), and by the Faith and Order Commission ("Scripture, Tradition, and Traditions" [Montreal, 1963], in *The Fourth World Conference on Faith and Order*, ed. P. C. Rodger and Lukas Vischer [New York: Association Press, 1964].) Important Lutheran studies are Gerhard Ebeling, *Wort Gottes und Tradition* (Göttingen: Vandenhoeck & Ruprecht, 1964), especially the section "'Sola Scriptura' und das Problem der Tradition," 91–143; Kristen E. Skydsgaard and Lukas Vischer, eds., *Schrift und Tradition* (WCC: Faith and Order Commission [Zurich: EVZ, 1963]), especially Skydsgaard, "Tradition und Wort Gottes," 128–156; G. Pedersen, "Bibliographie, 1930–1962," 157–69. Significant in Orthodox theology is Georges Florovsky, *Bible, Church, and Tradition: An Orthodox View*, vol. 1 of the Collected Works (Belmont, Mass.: Nordland Publishing Company, 1972). Seminal in Catholic theology are Josef Rupert Geiselmann, *Die lebendige Überlieferung als Norm des christlichen Glaubens* (Freiburg: Herder, 1958); George H. Tavard, *Holy Writ or Holy Church* (New York: Harper, 1959); and Yves Congar, *La*

Tradition et les traditions: Essai Historique (Paris: Librairie Arthème Fayard, 1960), and *La Tradition et les traditions: Essai Théologique* (Paris: Librairie Arthème Fayard, 1963).

5. L/RC 3, p. 197.
6. L/RC 4, p. 15.
7. L/RC 5, p. 22.
8. L/RC 6, p. 35.
9. Ibid.
10. L/RC 7, p. 74.
11. L/RC 8, p. 132.
12. FC SD 7:36; BC 575; BS 983; ELCA Const. 2.02a; DV 2–3.
13. Ap 12:53; BC 189; BS 261; ELCA Const. 2.02b; DV 1.
14. FC SD Rule and Norm 3; BC 503–4; BS 834; ELCA Const. 2.02c; DV 3–5.
15. ELCA Const. 2.2.03; DV 11, 24.
16. The process of tradition is compared with the universal experience of oral teaching "from father to son" in the controversies of the Counter-Reformation: George H. Tavard, *The Seventeenth-Century Tradition: A Study in Recusant Thought* (Leiden: Brill, 1978), 170–74.
17. See below, §§57–59.
18. *Summa theologiae*, Pt.I, q.l, a.10, ad 1.
19. This was Ockham's position; see Tavard, *Holy Writ or Holy Church*, 35–36.
20. The decisions of the Council of Constance (1414–18), which put an end to the Great Schism, were based on the conciliarist principle that an ecumenical council is superior to the pope. These decisions were ignored later, and there is a debate on their ecumenicity (Hans Küng, *Structures of the Church* [New York: Nelson, 1964], 268–88). For an overview of the literature, see Yves Congar, *L'Eglise de Saint Augustin à l'époque moderne* (Paris: Cerf, 1970), 305–38.
21. *Enarratio* is an approach to Scripture used in medieval work that involved essentially three steps: to explain the text (*narratio*); to take the message out of the text (*ex-narratio*); and to apply the message in public (*enarratio*).
22. Inge Lønning, "No Other Gospel: Luther's Concept of the 'Middle of Scripture' in Its Significance for Ecumenical Communion and Christian Confessions Today," in *Luther's Ecumenical Significance*, ed. Peter Manns and Harding Meyer (Philadelphia: Fortress, 1984), 229, 233–34. See also FC SD, Rule and Norm 1; BC 503–504; BS 834: the Scriptures are referred to as "the pure and clear fountain of Israel, which is the only true norm according to which all teachers and teachings are to be judged and evaluated."
23. LW 33:91; WA 18:653, 27.
24. LW 33:90; WA 18:653, 13–35.
25. LW 33:28; WA 18:609, 4–14.

26. LW 33:90; WA 18:653, 20.
27. LW 33:91; WA 18:653, 25. See the discussion in Friedrich Beisser, *Claritas Scripturae bei Martin Luther* (Göttingen: Vandenhoeck & Ruprecht, 1966), 83–97.
28. "Everything in the universe of Luther's Reformation stands or falls with the thesis of the clarity of Holy Scripture. That Christian theology is substantially bound to the task of interpretation of Scripture; that is, that it grows out of the struggle to resolve this task and leads into the struggle concerning the constantly renewed resolution of this same task, all this can only be understood when the clarity thesis is presupposed. The same is true of the unprecedented theological concentration on the understanding of the central message of Scripture and the remarkable calmness with regard to the question of the limit of the canon of Scripture. The function of the thesis of the clarity of Scripture, however, is only properly recognized when the essential content has been somewhat correctly determined. For Luther it is not a question, as is later the case with Orthodox dogmatists, of the quality of transparency (*perspicuitas*), which statements of Scripture should in a specific way have. Rather, the expression *claritas scripturae* should be understood quite unambiguously from the contrast between light and darkness and the imagery associated with these two concepts." Lønning, "No Other Gospel," 233.
29. WA 7, 97, 16–29. See the essay by Walter Mostert, "Scriptura sacra sui ipsius interpres," *Lutherjahrbuch* 46 (1979):60–96.
30. FC SD, Rule and Norm 3, 10; BC 503–504; BS 834, 838.
31. FC Ep, Rule and Norm 7, 2, 5; BC 465; BS 769, 768.
32. FC SD 12:40; BC 636; BS 1099.
33. FC SD Rule and Norm 10; BC 504; BS 838.
34. Latin and English versions in *The Decrees of the Ecumenical Councils*, 2 vols., ed. Norman P. Tanner (Washington, D.C.: Georgetown University Press, 1990), 2:663. Translation modified.
35. ". . . *pari pietatis affectu ac reverentia*." The expression *pari pietatis affectu* derives from St. Basil, who referred not to two sources of revelation but to two modes of transmission (ta men . . . ta de . . . : *De spiritu sancto*, PG 32:188A). See Congar, *Tradition*, 47–48.
36. Tanner, *Decrees*, 663.
37. "I think that the Catholic cause may not only be maintained by Scripture, but also that it has the better standing precisely by Scripture alone" (William Rushmore, d. 1637, cited in Tavard, *Seventeenth-Century*, 163.)
38. Lønning, "No Other Gospel," 232.
39. DV 4.
40. DV 7, 11, 19.
41. DV 10.
42. DV 21.

43. DV 9.
44. DV 8.
45. DV 10.
46. CA, end of Part I; BC 47; BS 83 c–d.
47. Ap 14; BC 214–15; BS 296–97.
48. Ap 14:5; BC 214; BS 296.
49. DV 8; see Joseph Ratzinger, "The Transmission of Divine Revelation," *Commentary on the Documents of Vatican II,* 5 vols., ed. Herbert Vorgrimler (New York: Herder and Herder, 1969), 3:183–84.
50. Ap 28:7; BC 282; BS 398.
51. Ap 28:16; BC 283; BS 401.
52. Ap 28:17; BC 283–84; BS 401.
53. In his Quodlibetum 17, printed in 1523, Konrad Köllin ascribes to his nephew Ulrich the conclusion that "the Sacred Letters teach nothing," adding however, "This I would not say myself" (quoted in Tavard, *Holy Writ,* p. 135); for other expressions that seem to devalue the Scriptures, see *Holy Writ,* p. 116 (Prierias), p. 132 (Henry VIII), p. 133 (Eustache of Zichen), p. 134 (Cornelius Snecanus).
54. The issue of "certainty of faith," including the Lutheran emphasis on *claritas* and on the contrast of *certitudo* and *securitas* (L/RC 8, p. 127), and involving the Catholic emphasis on the church community, calls for further future discussion.
55. DV 10.
56. DV 21.
57. DV 8.
58. See Ratzinger, "The Transmission," 185–86; 191–92.
59. FC SD Rule and Norm 1; BC 503; BS 834; DV 21.
60. LC 1:84–86; BC 376; BS 581–82; SC 24.
61. Ap 15:42; BC 221; BS 305:42; SC 52; DV 21.
62. LC Preface; BC 361:17; BS 552; DV 24.
63. LC, 1:100–101; BC 379; BS 585–86; cf. SC 7; DV 21.
64. L/RC 8, p. 61.
65. The approved ritual of the church has often been seen as evidence for the beliefs reflected in that ritual. For example, Augustine in his debate with Julian of Eclanum used the practice of infant baptism to establish his doctrine of original sin. Many other examples from the early centuries are given by Geoffrey Wainwright, *Doxology: The Praise of God in Worship, Doctrine, and Life* (New York: Oxford, 1980), 218–35. He shows how Ignatius of Antioch, Irenaeus, Tertullian, Cyprian, Optatus of Milevis, Ambrose, and Prosper of Aquitaine, among others, used the practice of the church in prayer as a basis for holding the truth of doctrines that are reflected in that practice. The maxim "Legem credendi lex statuat supplicandi" in chapter 8 of the *Indiculus gratiae* (DS 246) is

generally attributed to Prosper of Aquitaine.

66. *Mediator Dei* (1947) 48; text in *The Papal Encyclicals*, 5 vols., ed. Claudia Carlen (Wilmington, N.C.: McGrath Publishing Company, 1981), 4:119–54, at 128.

67. Edmund Schlink points out that creeds partake of the structure of doxology and that dogma is a second-order language having its basis in worship and witness; *The Coming Christ and the Coming Church* (Philadelphia: Fortress, 1968), 16–84.

68. See Luther's *Forma missae et communionis* of 1523 and his *Deutsche Messe* of 1526 for the removal of sacrificial language from the Mass. See Wainwright, *Doxology*, 268–69.

69. For example, faithful Protestants protested against the Nazi-inspired "German Christian" movement in the Barmen Declaration of 1934. Confessional language is likewise present in the encyclical of Pius XI, *Mit brennender Sorge* (1937; text in *AAS* [1937]:145–67), with its prophetic warnings against the idolatrous cult of race and state.

70. See *LWF Report* 19/20 (1985):179–80. In taking this action in 1984, the Seventh Assembly of the LWF reaffirmed the statement against apartheid of the sixth assembly (Dar es Salaam, 1977).

71. UR 12.

72. UR 20.

73. The pope, addressing representatives of the Council of the German Evangelical Church at Mainz on November 17, 1980, is here quoting with approval a pastoral letter of the German bishops issued on January 20, 1980, in connection with the 450th anniversary of the Augsburg Confession. The text of the pope's address in German may be found in AAS 73 (1981):71–75, at 73. For the English translation see *LWF Report* 10 (1980), Document 9, pp. 62–66, at 64; also *Information Service* of the Secretariat for Promoting Christian Unity, 45 (1981):5–7, at 6. The pastoral letter of the German bishops is printed in *LWF Report* 10, Document 6, p. 55.

74. For some proposed steps toward reconciliation see *The Condemnations of the Reformation Era: Do They Still Divide?*, ed. Karl Lehmann and Wolfhart Pannenberg (Minneapolis: Fortress, 1990). Dealing primarily with the condemnations of the Council of Trent and those of the Formula of Concord, this report, issued by a Joint Ecumenical Commission in Germany, concludes: "A whole series of sixteenth-century condemnatory pronouncements rested on misunderstandings about the opposite position. Others were directed at extreme positions that were not binding on the church. Again, others do not apply to today's partner" (p. 27). But the report acknowledges also that in some disputed matters, possibly not church-dividing, the dialogue group was unable to establish a sufficient consensus. It declared: "There is as yet no explicit consensus about the critical function of Scripture over against the formation of the church's tradition" (ibid.).

75. These "ecumenical" creeds are printed at the beginning of the Lutheran Book of Concord and appear in standard collections of Catholic official teaching, such as Denzinger-Schönmetzer. The "Athanasian" creed (*Quicumque*), at least today, does not enjoy as high a doctrinal and liturgical status in the practice of our churches as do the other two.

76. Letter *De Decretis nicaenae synodi*, PG 25:451; cf. John Courtney Murray in L/RC 1, p. 17.

77. FC SD, Rule and Norm 2; BC 504; BS 834.

78. "Summary Statement," L/RC 1, p. 32, §6a. The statement acknowledged in §6c: "The way in which doctrine is certified as dogma is not identical in the two communities, for there is a difference in the way in which mutually acknowledged doctrine receives ecclesiastical sanction" (ibid.).

79. In the words of George Lindbeck quoted by Warren A. Quanbeck, "The church is obligated to a continuous search (in reliance on the Holy Spirit and with the help of reason) for fuller understanding of what faithfulness to the scriptural witness involves." See his "The Second Theological Consultation between Lutherans and Catholics" in L/RC 2, p. 76.

80. UR 6; Congregation for the Doctrine of the Faith, *Mysterium Ecclesiae*, AAS 65 (1973):396–408, esp. no. 5, pp. 402–404.

81. Cf. International Theological Commission, "On the Interpretation of Dogmas," *Origins* 20 (May 17, 1990):1–14, at 10.

82. See L/RC 8, p. 88, "Common Statement" no. 164, with note 149, p. 352.

83. The numbers in parentheses refer to the English translation, *The Dogma of the Assumption* (New York: Paulist, 1951). The official text is found in *AAS* 42 (1950): no. 26, p. 762; no. 20, p. 760; no. 41, p. 769. Around the time of the definition a considerable amount of literature was published on the theme of the progress of dogma. See, e.g., Clément Dillenschneider, *Le sens de la foi et le progrès dogmatique du mystère marial* (Rome: Academia Mariana Internationalis, 1954). See also Avery Dulles, "The Dogma of the Assumption," L/RC 8, pp. 279–94.

84. The term is attributed to Georg Calixt (d. 1656). See J. Wallmann in TRE 7 (1981):554. In an early translation of the *Book of Concord*, vol. 2, Historical Introduction, Appendices and Indexes, ed. Henry E. Jacobs (Philadelphia: General Council Publication Board, 1883), Calovius, as quoted in "Catalogue of Testimonies," was included, pp. 272–93.

85. Heinrich Schmid, *The Doctrinal Theology of the Evangelical Lutheran Church* (3rd ed., rev., translated from German and Latin; Minneapolis: Augsburg, 1899, reprinted 1961), 95.

86. L/RC 8, p. 55.

87. See "Catholic and Lutheran Reflections" in L/RC 6, pp. 38–68.

88. LG 25.

89. CA 28:5–8, 21–22; BC 81–82, 84; BS 121–22, 123–24.

90. Ap 7–8:5; BC 169; BS 234–35; *Small Catechism* 3:6; BC 345; BS 511–12; DV 5 and 8.

91. UR 14, 17; AG 22.

92. DV 8; LG 12; cf. LG 25; also Jn 14:25–26; 16:22–23.

93. The Catholic understanding of *sensus fidei*, in contrast to mere public opinion, is explained in the Congregation for the Doctrine of the Faith's *Instruction on the Ecclesial Vocation of the Theologian*, no. 35; text in *Origins* 20 (July 5, 1990):117–26, at 124. See also John Paul II, Apostolic Exhortation *Familiaris consortio*, no. 5; text in *Origins* 11 (December 24, 1981):437–68, at 440.

94. L/RC 6, p. 67.

List of Participants

CATHOLICS

The Rev. Avery Dulles, S.J.
Fordham University, Bronx, New York
The Rev. Robert B. Eno, S.S.
Catholic University of America, Washington, D.C.
The Rev. Joseph A. Fitzmyer, S.J.
Georgetown University, Washington, D.C.
Sr. Elizabeth A. Johnson, C.S.J.
Fordham University, Bronx, New York
The Rev. Kilian McDonnell, O.S.B.
Institute for Ecumenical and Cultural Research, Collegeville, Minnesota
The Rev. Walter Principe, C.S.B.
Pontifical Institute of Mediaeval Studies, Toronto, Ontario/ University of Toronto, Toronto, Ontario
The Most Rev. J. Francis Stafford (Co-chair)
Bishop, Archdiocese of Denver, Colorado
The Rev. Georges H. Tavard, A.A.
Brighton, Massachusetts
The Rev. Frederick M. Jelly, O.P. (Consultant)
Mount St. Mary's Seminary, Emmitsburg, Maryland
The Rev. John F. Hotchkin (Staff)
Bishops' Committee for Ecumenical and Interreligious Affairs, Washington, D.C.

61

LCMS Participants

Dr. John Franklin Johnson
  Concordia Seminary, St. Louis, Missouri
Dr. John Frederick Johnson
  Inter-Lutheran Council for Continuing Education, St. Petersburg, Florida
Dr. David G. Schmiel
  Theological Education Services, LCMS, St. Louis, Missouri
Dr. Samuel H. Nafzger (Staff)
  Commission on Theology and Church Relations, LCMS, St. Louis, Missouri

ELCA Participants

Dr. Robert W. Bertram
  St. Louis, Missouri
Dr. Joseph A. Burgess
  Regent, North Dakota
Dr. Gerhard O. Forde
  Luther Seminary, St. Paul, Minnesota
Dr. Karlfried Froehlich
  Princeton Theological Seminary, Princeton, New Jersey
Dr. Eric Gritsch
  Lutheran Theological Seminary, Gettysburg, Pennsylvania
Dr. Kenneth Hagen
  Marquette University, Milwaukee, Wisconsin
Dr. Winston D. Persaud
  Wartburg Theological Seminary, Dubuque, Iowa
Dr. John Reumann
  Lutheran Theological Seminary, Philadelphia, Pennsylvania
Dr. Harold C. Skillrud (Co-chair)
  Bishop, ELCA Southeastern Synod, Atlanta, Georgia
Dr. Daniel F. Martensen (Staff)
  Department for Ecumenical Affairs, ELCA, Chicago, Illinois